THE ART OF WEALTH MASTERY: UNLOCKING ABUNDANCE IN YOUR LIFE

Introduction: Unlocking Your Path to Abundance

Welcome, dear reader, to a transformative journey towards mastering the art of wealth and unlocking abundance in your life. This book is not just about money; it is a comprehensive guide designed to empower you with the mindset, strategies, and practical techniques necessary to achieve financial success and create a life of true wealth.

In a world that often measures success by material possessions and monetary gains, it is easy to lose sight of the deeper meaning of wealth. True wealth encompasses more than just financial prosperity; it embraces the richness of experiences, meaningful relationships, personal growth, and making a positive impact on the world around us.

This journey begins by understanding the true meaning of wealth and challenging the limiting beliefs that have held you back. It is about shifting your mindset from scarcity to abundance, cultivating a positive relationship with money, and harnessing the extraordinary power of visualization and affirmations to manifest wealth and abundance in your life.

Building upon this foundation, we delve into the practical aspects of wealth creation. We explore the importance of establishing a solid financial foundation, setting clear goals, budgeting effectively, and creating multiple streams of income. We uncover the world of investments, understand the psychology of wise financial decisions, and develop an entrepreneurial mindset to embrace opportunities and overcome obstacles.

But this journey is not just about accumulating wealth; it is about creating a life of purpose, balance, and fulfillment. We dive into cultivating a wealthy lifestyle that encompasses personal well-being, sustainable wealth planning, and giving back to the community. We navigate the challenges, setbacks, and financial risks with resilience and perseverance, staying motivated on the path to financial freedom.

Throughout this book, you will find practical strategies, real-life examples, and inspiring stories of individuals who have achieved financial abundance. You will discover the power of networking and nurturing relationships, harness the psychology of success, and create a personal brand that positions you as an authority in your field.

Each chapter is an invitation to explore, learn, and take actionable steps towards your financial goals. It is a reminder that you have the power to create the life of abundance you desire, one that aligns with your values, passions, and aspirations.

So, dear reader, I invite you to embark on this empowering journey with an open mind and a willingness to embrace change. Let go of limitations, envision a future of abundance, and ignite the flame of motivation within you. The path to wealth mastery awaits, and you have the power to unlock the abundant life you deserve.

Together, let us delve into the art of wealth mastery and unlock the extraordinary possibilities that lie ahead. Your journey to abundance starts now.

CONTENTS

CHAPTER 1: INTRODUCTION: THE PATH TO PROSPERITY

"Success is not the key to happiness. Happiness is the key to success. If you love what you are doing, you will be successful." - Albert Schweitzer

Introduction: Welcome, dear reader, to the enlightening journey towards mastering the art of wealth and unlocking abundance in your life. This chapter serves as the gateway to your path to prosperity, where we will explore the true meaning of wealth and overcome the limiting beliefs that have hindered your financial success.

Understanding the True Meaning of Wealth:

To embark on this transformative journey, it is crucial to have a clear understanding of what wealth truly entails. Wealth extends far beyond mere monetary possessions; it encompasses every facet of a fulfilling and prosperous life. True wealth encompasses financial prosperity, a healthy mind and body, fulfilling relationships, personal growth, and making a positive impact on the world around us.

So, let us set our sights on a holistic definition of wealth that incorporates all these aspects. Wealth means having an abundance of financial resources to live comfortably, pursuing our passions, and enjoying the experiences that enrich our lives.

It means having the freedom and flexibility to spend quality time with loved ones and nurturing meaningful relationships. Wealth also encompasses having a purpose-driven life, continuously learning and growing, and giving back to the community.

Overcoming Limiting Beliefs about Money:

One of the most significant hurdles on the path to wealth mastery lies within our own minds. Many of us carry deep-rooted limiting beliefs about money, which act as barriers to our financial success. These beliefs can manifest as thoughts such as "Money is scarce," "Money is evil," or "I don't deserve to be wealthy."

To break free from these self-imposed limitations, we must first recognize and challenge these beliefs. Start by acknowledging that money is a neutral tool that can be used for both positive and negative purposes. Embrace the belief that you have the potential to create and attract wealth through your talents, skills, and dedicated efforts. Replace scarcity with abundance, and see money as a means to enhance your life and make a positive impact on others.

Real-Life Strategies and Helpful Techniques:

1. Affirmations and Visualization: Harness the power of your subconscious mind by practicing affirmations and visualization. Affirmations are positive statements that you repeat daily to reprogram your mind with empowering beliefs about money and abundance. Visualize yourself already living the life of wealth and abundance you desire, engaging your senses to make the experience vivid and compelling.

2. Surround Yourself with Abundance: Create an environment that supports your wealth mindset. Surround yourself with positive and successful individuals who inspire and uplift you. Immerse yourself in educational resources, books, and podcasts that expand your financial knowledge and broaden your perspectives. As the saying goes, "You are the average of

the five people you spend the most time with."

3. Continuous Learning: Commit yourself to lifelong learning. Expand your knowledge of personal finance, investing and wealth-building strategies. Attend seminars, workshops, and conferences to gain insights from experts in the field. Cultivate a thirst for knowledge and a growth mindset that embraces new opportunities and challenges.

4. Take Inspired Action: Knowledge alone is not enough; action is the catalyst for transformation. Set clear financial goals and create actionable plans to achieve them. Break down your goals into smaller, manageable steps, and take consistent action towards their realization. Remember, progress is made one step at a time.

5. Embrace a Spirit of Gratitude: Gratitude is the foundation of abundance. Cultivate a daily gratitude practice, acknowledging the blessings and abundance already present in your life. When you appreciate what you have, you attract more positive experiences and opportunities for wealth.

6. Seek Mentors and Role Models: Identify mentors and role models who have achieved the financial success you aspire to. Learn from their experiences, seek their guidance, and model their strategies. A mentor can provide valuable insights, support, and accountability on your wealth-building journey.

In Conclusion:

Dear reader, as we conclude this first chapter, I urge you to reflect upon the true meaning of wealth and challenge the limiting beliefs that may have held you back. By understanding the expansive nature of wealth and adopting a mindset of abundance, you are laying the foundation for your journey towards financial prosperity.

Implement the strategies and techniques shared here, and remember that true success comes not only from monetary gains but from finding joy and fulfillment in the pursuit of your passions. Embrace the path to prosperity with open arms and an unwavering belief in your ability to create abundance in every area of your life.

May this chapter be the catalyst that ignites your journey towards mastering the art of wealth and unlocking the abundance that awaits you.

CHAPTER 2: THE WEALTH MINDSET: CULTIVATING ABUNDANCE

"Whatever the mind can conceive and believe, it can achieve." - Napoleon Hill

Introduction: Greetings, dear reader, as we embark on the transformative journey of cultivating a wealth mindset. In this chapter, we will explore the extraordinary power of shifting from a scarcity mindset to an abundance mindset. We will delve into strategies and techniques that will help you develop a positive relationship with money, harness the incredible tools of visualization and affirmations, and manifest wealth and abundance in your life.

Shifting Your Mindset from Scarcity to Abundance:

To embark on the path of wealth mastery, we must first liberate ourselves from the constraints of a scarcity mindset. The scarcity mindset is rooted in the false belief that there is a limited amount of wealth, success, and opportunities available in the world. It breeds fear, anxiety, and a constant sense of lack.

However, the truth is that the universe is abundant, and there is an unlimited supply of wealth and opportunities for those who choose to embrace an abundance mindset. Abundance thinking is grounded in the belief that there is more than enough to go around, and that as we create and share wealth, it multiplies for everyone.

To shift from a scarcity mindset to an abundance mindset, start by consciously choosing thoughts and beliefs that support abundance. Replace thoughts of lack with thoughts of plenty. Affirm to yourself that there is an abundance of wealth, opportunities, and resources available for you to tap into. Embrace a mindset of gratitude for the wealth that already exists in your life, and trust that more will flow to you as you align your thoughts, beliefs, and actions with abundance.

Developing a Positive Relationship with Money:

Money, dear reader, is a powerful tool that can enable us to live fulfilling lives, pursue our passions, and make a positive impact in the world. It is essential to cultivate a positive relationship with money in order to attract and create wealth. Here are some strategies and techniques to help you develop a healthy and empowering relationship with money:

1. Gratitude and Appreciation: Express gratitude for the money you currently possess and the financial blessings in your life. Develop a genuine appreciation for the abundance that money brings and the opportunities it provides. The more you appreciate what you have, the more the universe will bring forth opportunities for you to experience greater wealth.

2. Shift from Fear to Trust: Release any fears or anxieties you may have around money, and replace them with trust. Trust in your ability to create wealth, attract financial opportunities, and manage your finances wisely. Trust that the universe will provide for your needs as you align your actions with your financial goals.

3. Focus on Value Creation: Instead of solely focusing on making money, shift your focus to creating value for

others. Seek to provide products, services, or solutions that genuinely benefit and improve the lives of others. As you focus on creating value, the money will naturally flow to you as a result of the positive impact you have on others.

Exploring the Power of Visualization and Affirmations:

Visualization and affirmations are potent tools that can reprogram your subconscious mind and align your thoughts and beliefs with your desires. These techniques allow you to harness the creative power of your mind and attract wealth and abundance into your life. Here are practical strategies to help you utilize visualization and affirmations effectively:

1. Visualization: Set aside dedicated time each day to engage in visualization. Close your eyes and vividly imagine yourself already living the life of abundance you desire. Visualize your bank account growing, see yourself achieving your financial goals, and feel the emotions of joy, abundance, and fulfillment as you imagine living a prosperous life. Engage all your senses to make the visualization experience as vivid and real as possible.

2. Affirmations: Craft powerful affirmations that align with your wealth goals and repeat them daily with conviction and belief. Affirmations such as "I am worthy of abundant wealth," "I attract limitless financial opportunities," and "Money flows to me effortlessly and abundantly" reinforce your positive mindset and program your subconscious mind for success. Repeat these affirmations aloud or silently, and truly embody the feelings and emotions associated with each affirmation.

Real-Life Strategies and Helpful Techniques:

1. Create a Vision Board: Visual representation is a potent tool for manifestation. Create a vision board by

collecting images, words, and symbols that represent the abundance you seek. Place the vision board somewhere visible, such as your bedroom or office, and spend a few moments each day focusing on it. Allow the images to evoke positive emotions and reinforce your belief in your ability to attract and create wealth.

2. Surround Yourself with Abundance: Surround yourself with physical reminders of abundance. Display books on wealth creation, artwork that represents prosperity, or even a jar filled with coins or bills. These tangible representations will serve as constant reminders of your wealth goals and keep you aligned with the vibration of abundance.

3. Practice Daily Gratitude: Cultivate a daily gratitude practice focused specifically on your financial situation. Take a few moments each day to express gratitude for the money you have, the opportunities you've received, and the wealth that is flowing into your life. This practice will amplify your abundance mindset and attract more financial blessings.

4. Engage in Positive Self-Talk: Monitor your thoughts and ensure that they align with abundance and wealth. Replace any negative or limiting self-talk about money with positive and empowering statements. Remind yourself that you are worthy of financial abundance, and affirm that you have the power to create wealth in your life. Adopt an inner dialogue that supports your wealth goals and encourages your success.

5. Seek Financial Education: Commit to lifelong learning about personal finance, investments, and wealth-building strategies. Attend seminars, read books written by financial experts, listen to podcasts, and surround yourself with individuals who have achieved financial success. Education will empower you with the

knowledge and confidence necessary to navigate your wealth journey effectively.

In Conclusion:

Congratulations, dear reader, on embarking on the path to cultivating a wealth mindset! By shifting your mindset from scarcity to abundance, developing a positive relationship with money, and utilizing powerful tools like visualization and affirmations, you are actively creating the foundation for a life of financial abundance.

Remember, your thoughts and beliefs shape your reality. Embrace the power within you to attract wealth and abundance, and watch as the universe aligns with your intentions. Stay committed to your wealth mindset journey, and trust that the universe will conspire to bring you the prosperity you seek.

CHAPTER 3: BUILDING A SOLID FINANCIAL FOUNDATION

"Financial freedom is available to those who learn about it and work for it." - Robert Kiyosaki

Introduction: Welcome, dear reader, to the enlightening chapter dedicated to building a solid financial foundation. In this chapter, we will explore the fundamental principles and practical strategies necessary to establish a strong financial footing. By laying a solid foundation, you will gain control over your finances, create stability, and set yourself up for long-term wealth accumulation.

Understanding Your Current Financial Situation: To build a solid financial foundation, it is essential to have a clear understanding of your current financial situation. Let's explore the steps to gain a comprehensive overview:

1. Assess Your Income and Expenses: Begin by analyzing your income sources and calculating your total monthly income. Next, track your expenses for at least a month to determine where your money is going. Categorize your expenses into essential (e.g., housing, utilities, groceries) and discretionary (e.g., entertainment, dining out). This assessment will help you identify areas where you can potentially cut back and optimize your spending.

2. Calculate Your Net Worth: Determine your net worth by subtracting your liabilities (e.g., debts, loans) from your assets (e.g., savings, investments, property). This calculation provides a snapshot of your financial health and serves as a starting point for your wealth-building journey.

3. Review Your Debts: Examine your outstanding debts, including credit card balances, student loans, and personal loans. Note the interest rates, monthly payments, and remaining balances for each debt. Understanding your debt obligations is crucial for creating a plan to manage and eliminate them effectively.

Establishing a Budget: Once you have a clear understanding of your financial situation, the next step is to establish a budget. A budget is a powerful tool that helps you allocate your income effectively and ensures that your spending aligns with your financial goals. Here's how to create a budget:

1. Determine Your Financial Goals: Set short-term and long-term financial goals. These goals may include building an emergency fund, paying off debt, saving for a down payment on a house, or investing for retirement. Having clear goals allows you to prioritize your spending and make informed financial decisions.

2. Track Your Income and Expenses: Monitor your income and expenses regularly. Use tools such as spreadsheets, budgeting apps, or online platforms to track your financial inflows and outflows accurately. This tracking enables you to identify areas where you may be overspending and make adjustments accordingly.

3. Allocate Your Income: Divide your income into categories such as essential expenses (e.g., housing, utilities, transportation), savings, debt repayment, and discretionary spending. Allocate a specific portion of

your income to each category based on your financial goals and priorities.

4. Regularly Review and Adjust: Review your budget regularly and make adjustments as needed. Life circumstances and financial goals may change, requiring modifications to your spending allocations. Be flexible and proactive in managing your budget to ensure its effectiveness.

Emergency Fund and Insurance: Building an emergency fund and obtaining adequate insurance coverage are essential components of a solid financial foundation. Let's explore these aspects in more detail:

1. Establish an Emergency Fund: An emergency fund acts as a safety net for unexpected financial emergencies, such as medical expenses, car repairs, or job loss. Aim to save three to six months' worth of living expenses in a separate, easily accessible account. Start small and gradually build your emergency fund over time, focusing on consistency and discipline.

2. Obtain Adequate Insurance Coverage: Insurance provides protection against various risks, such as health issues, accidents, property damage, or liability. Assess your insurance needs and secure policies that align with your circumstances. This may include health insurance, life insurance, disability insurance, auto insurance, home insurance, or business insurance. Adequate coverage helps mitigate potential financial losses and provides peace of mind.

Eliminating Debt and Building Wealth: To solidify your financial foundation, it is crucial to eliminate debt and focus on building wealth. Here are strategies to help you achieve these goals:

1. Implement Debt Repayment Strategies: Prioritize paying off high-interest debts first, such as credit card balances. Consider strategies like the debt snowball

or debt avalanche method mentioned in Chapter 6 to accelerate your debt repayment journey. Make consistent payments and avoid taking on new debt whenever possible.

2. Save and Invest: Allocate a portion of your income to savings and investments. Set up automatic transfers to savings accounts or investment vehicles such as retirement accounts or brokerage accounts. Start with small contributions and gradually increase them over time. Investing in diversified assets allows your money to grow and work for you in the long term.

3. Educate Yourself on Personal Finance and Investing: Continuously expand your knowledge of personal finance and investment strategies. Read books, listen to podcasts, attend workshops, and seek advice from reputable financial professionals. Educating yourself empowers you to make informed decisions and maximize your financial opportunities.

4. Seek Professional Advice: Consider consulting with a financial advisor or planner to get personalized guidance on your financial journey. A professional can help you navigate complex financial decisions, provide tailored strategies, and offer valuable insights based on their expertise and experience.

In Conclusion: Congratulations, dear reader, on taking the crucial steps toward building a solid financial foundation. By understanding your current financial situation, establishing a budget, creating an emergency fund, obtaining adequate insurance coverage, eliminating debt, and focusing on building wealth, you are setting yourself up for long-term financial success. Remember, building a solid financial foundation requires discipline, patience, and a commitment to your financial goals. Stay dedicated to your journey, adapt as circumstances change, and continue to educate yourself on personal finance and wealth-building strategies. With a solid foundation in place, you will have the stability and resources necessary to pursue your dreams, enjoy financial freedom, and create a life of abundance.

CHAPTER 4: GENERATING MULTIPLE STREAMS OF INCOME

"Never depend on a single income. Make investments to create a second source." - Warren Buffett

Introduction: Welcome, dear reader, to the enlightening chapter dedicated to generating multiple streams of income. In this chapter, we will explore the power of diversifying your income sources and leveraging your skills and passions to create financial abundance. By developing multiple streams of income, you can increase your earning potential, build wealth faster, and achieve financial independence.

Identifying and Leveraging Your Skills and Passions: To generate multiple streams of income, it is essential to identify your unique skills, talents, and passions. Take some time for self-reflection and exploration to discover what you excel at and what brings you joy. Here are some strategies to help you in this process:

1. Self-Assessment: Reflect on your strengths, talents, and areas of expertise. Consider your professional skills, hobbies, and interests. Identify any gaps or areas where you can acquire additional skills or knowledge to enhance your income-generating potential.

2. Passion and Purpose: Identify activities or industries that ignite your passion and align with your values. When you pursue activities you genuinely enjoy, you are more likely to find success and fulfillment. Explore opportunities to turn your passions into income-generating ventures.

3. Market Demand: Research and identify industries or areas that have a high demand for specific skills or products. Look for gaps in the market that you can fill with your expertise or unique offerings. By providing solutions to existing needs, you increase your income potential.

Exploring Various Income-Generating Opportunities: Once you have identified your skills and passions, it's time to explore various income-generating opportunities. Here are some avenues to consider:

1. Employment or Business: Consider traditional employment opportunities in your field of expertise. Alternatively, explore the possibility of starting your own business or freelancing. Entrepreneurship offers the freedom to pursue your passions, control your income, and potentially scale your business for greater financial success.

2. Side Hustles: Side hustles are additional income-generating activities that you pursue alongside your primary source of income. These can include gig economy jobs, online freelancing, consulting, tutoring, or selling products or services online. Side hustles provide flexibility and can be a stepping stone toward creating a full-time business if desired.

3. Rental Income: If you have the means, consider investing in real estate properties for rental income. This can involve residential properties, commercial spaces, or even vacation rentals. Rental income provides

a steady cash flow and the potential for long-term wealth accumulation through property appreciation.

4. Investments: Explore investment opportunities that generate passive income. This can include stocks, bonds, mutual funds, or dividend-paying assets. Real estate investment trusts (REITs), peer-to-peer lending, or investing in startups through crowdfunding platforms are other options to consider.

Creating Passive Income Streams: Passive income streams allow you to earn money with minimal ongoing effort or time investment. Here are some passive income ideas to explore:

1. Rental Properties: As mentioned earlier, real estate investments can provide passive rental income when managed properly. Consider hiring a property management company to handle day-to-day operations, making it a more passive endeavor.

2. Dividend-Paying Stocks: Invest in stocks that offer regular dividend payments. Dividends are a portion of a company's profits distributed to shareholders, providing a consistent stream of income.

3. Royalties: If you possess creative skills, such as writing, music, or photography, explore opportunities to earn royalties from your work. This can include publishing books, licensing music, or selling stock photos.

4. Online Courses or Digital Products: Create and sell online courses, e-books, or other digital products. Once developed, these products can generate passive income as they can be sold repeatedly without significant additional effort.

Strategies for Long-Term Wealth Accumulation: While generating multiple streams of income is a powerful wealth-building strategy, it is equally important to focus on long-term wealth accumulation. Here are some strategies to consider:

1. Save and Invest Wisely: As you increase your income from multiple sources, ensure you have a disciplined approach to saving and investing. Allocate a portion of your income toward savings and investment accounts to build wealth over time.

2. Diversify Your Investments: Similar to diversifying your income streams, diversify your investment portfolio. Invest in a mix of assets, such as stocks, bonds, real estate, and commodities, to spread the risk and maximize potential returns.

3. Set Clear Financial Goals: Establish specific financial goals that align with your desired lifestyle and aspirations. Whether it's saving for retirement, buying a home, or funding your children's education, having clear goals provides direction and motivation for long-term wealth accumulation.

4. Continuously Learn and Adapt: Stay updated on industry trends, market changes, and new income-generating opportunities. The world is constantly evolving, and by embracing a growth mindset and adapting to new opportunities, you can stay ahead and ensure continued financial success.

In Conclusion: Congratulations, dear reader, on exploring the power of generating multiple streams of income. By identifying and leveraging your skills and passions, exploring various income-generating opportunities, and creating passive income streams, you are expanding your earning potential and setting yourself up for financial abundance.

Remember, generating multiple streams of income requires effort, dedication, and a willingness to explore new opportunities. Be open to learning, adapt as needed, and stay committed to your long-term financial goals. As your income diversifies, ensure you have a well-thought-out savings and investment strategy to maximize your wealth accumulation and create a life of financial freedom.

May your journey toward multiple streams of income be filled with abundance and success.

CHAPTER 5: MASTERING INVESTMENTS AND WEALTH CREATION

"The stock market is filled with individuals who know the price of everything but the value of nothing." - Philip Fisher

Introduction: Welcome, dear reader, to the insightful chapter dedicated to mastering investments and wealth creation. In this chapter, we will explore the fundamentals of investing, the various investment vehicles available, and the strategies for long-term wealth accumulation. By mastering the art of investing, you can harness the power of wealth creation and build a solid financial future.

Understanding the Basics of Investing: Before diving into specific investment vehicles, it is crucial to grasp the basics of investing. Investing involves allocating your financial resources with the expectation of generating returns or profits over time. Here are some key concepts to understand:

1. Risk and Return: Investments inherently involve risk. The general principle is that higher-risk investments have the potential for higher returns, but also a greater chance of losses. It is essential to assess your risk

tolerance and align it with your investment strategy.

2. Time Horizon: Consider your investment time horizon, which refers to the length of time you plan to hold an investment before needing the funds. Longer time horizons generally allow for more aggressive investment strategies, while shorter time horizons may require a more conservative approach.

3. Diversification: Diversification is the practice of spreading your investments across different asset classes, industries, and geographic regions. This helps mitigate risk by reducing the impact of a single investment's performance on your overall portfolio.

Exploring Different Investment Vehicles: Now, let's explore some common investment vehicles you can consider as part of your wealth creation journey:

1. Stocks: Stocks represent ownership shares in publicly traded companies. Investing in stocks allows you to participate in a company's growth and potentially benefit from capital appreciation and dividends. Research and analyze companies before investing, considering factors such as their financial health, industry outlook, and competitive advantage.

2. Bonds: Bonds are debt securities issued by governments, municipalities, and corporations. When you purchase a bond, you are essentially lending money to the issuer in exchange for regular interest payments and the return of the principal amount at maturity. Bonds are generally considered lower-risk investments compared to stocks.

3. Real Estate: Real estate investments can involve purchasing properties for rental income or capital appreciation. Real estate can provide both ongoing cash flow through rental income and the potential for long-term value appreciation. Options include residential properties, commercial properties, real

estate investment trusts (REITs), and real estate crowdfunding platforms.

4. Mutual Funds and Exchange-Traded Funds (ETFs): Mutual funds and ETFs pool money from multiple investors to invest in a diversified portfolio of securities. These investment vehicles offer convenience and professional management. Mutual funds are actively managed, while ETFs typically passively track an index.

5. Commodities: Commodities include tangible goods such as gold, silver, oil, natural gas, agricultural products, and more. Investing in commodities can provide a hedge against inflation and diversification benefits. However, commodity investments can be volatile and may require specific knowledge and expertise.

Strategies for Long-Term Wealth Accumulation: Building wealth through investments requires a thoughtful approach and long-term perspective. Here are strategies to consider for long-term wealth accumulation:

1. Set Clear Investment Goals: Define your investment goals based on your financial objectives, risk tolerance, and time horizon. Establish goals such as wealth preservation, retirement planning, funding education, or achieving financial independence. Clear goals will guide your investment decisions and asset allocation.

2. Dollar-Cost Averaging: Implement a dollar-cost averaging strategy by investing a fixed amount regularly over time, regardless of market conditions. This approach reduces the impact of short-term market volatility and allows you to benefit from the potential long-term growth of your investments.

3. Rebalance Your Portfolio: Regularly review and rebalance your investment portfolio to maintain your desired asset allocation. Market fluctuations may cause your portfolio to deviate from your original allocation.

Rebalancing ensures that you are not overly exposed to certain investments and helps manage risk.

4. Stay Informed and Educated: Stay updated on market trends, economic indicators, and investment news. Continuously educate yourself about investing strategies, financial markets, and the performance of your investment holdings. This knowledge empowers you to make informed decisions and adapt to changing market conditions.

5. Seek Professional Guidance: Consider working with a financial advisor or investment professional to develop a personalized investment strategy. A professional can provide expert guidance, help you navigate complex investment decisions, and ensure your portfolio aligns with your long-term goals.

In Conclusion: Congratulations, dear reader, on exploring the art of investing and wealth creation. By understanding the basics of investing, exploring different investment vehicles, and implementing strategies for long-term wealth accumulation, you are on the path to financial success.

Remember, investing requires patience, discipline, and a long-term perspective. Regularly assess your investment goals, diversify your portfolio, and stay informed about market trends. Seek professional guidance when needed and continuously educate yourself about investing strategies and financial markets.

May your journey of mastering investments be filled with wise decisions, fruitful returns, and the realization of your long-term financial goals.

CHAPTER 6:
NAVIGATING DEBT
AND FINANCIAL RISKS

"Before you can become a millionaire, you must learn to think like one. You must learn how to motivate yourself to counter fear with courage." - Thomas J. Stanley

Introduction: Welcome, dear reader, to the insightful chapter dedicated to navigating debt and financial risks. In this chapter, we will explore the importance of managing debt effectively, mitigating financial risks, and protecting your assets. By understanding and addressing these aspects, you can safeguard your financial well-being and pave the way for long-term wealth accumulation.

Managing and Reducing Debt Effectively: Debt management plays a crucial role in achieving financial stability and building wealth. It is essential to approach debt with a strategic mindset and develop a plan to reduce and eliminate it. Here are strategies for managing and reducing debt effectively:

1. Assess Your Debt: Begin by taking stock of your existing debts. Make a list of all your debts, including credit card balances, student loans, mortgages, and personal loans. Note the interest rates, monthly payments, and remaining balances for each debt.

2. Prioritize High-Interest Debt: Focus on paying off high-interest debts first, as they tend to cost you more in the long run. Allocate more of your available funds toward these debts while making minimum payments on other lower-interest debts.

3. Debt Snowball Method: Consider using the debt snowball method, where you pay off the smallest debts first while making minimum payments on larger debts. As each smaller debt is paid off, you can redirect the funds to tackle the next smallest debt, creating a snowball effect and gaining momentum.

4. Debt Avalanche Method: Alternatively, you can follow the debt avalanche method, which prioritizes paying off debts with the highest interest rates first. This approach saves you more money on interest payments in the long term.

5. Consolidate and Refinance: Explore options for consolidating your debts or refinancing high-interest loans to obtain lower interest rates. This can simplify your payments and potentially save you money on interest charges.

Mitigating Financial Risks and Protecting Your Assets: Protecting your financial well-being involves mitigating potential risks and safeguarding your assets. Here are strategies to consider:

1. Emergency Fund: Build an emergency fund to handle unexpected expenses or financial setbacks. Aim to save three to six months' worth of living expenses in an easily accessible account. Having this safety net helps mitigate the need to rely on credit or go into further debt during emergencies.

2. Insurance Coverage: Assess your insurance needs and ensure you have adequate coverage to protect yourself and your assets. This can include health insurance, life insurance, disability insurance, auto insurance, home

insurance, or business insurance. Carefully review policy terms, coverage limits, and deductibles to ensure you are adequately protected.

3. Estate Planning: Develop an estate plan that outlines how your assets will be managed and distributed in the event of your incapacity or passing. This may include creating a will, establishing trusts, designating beneficiaries, and selecting a power of attorney or healthcare proxy. Estate planning helps protect your assets and ensures your wishes are carried out.

4. Risk Management: Regularly assess and manage risks associated with your investments and financial decisions. Diversify your investment portfolio, conduct thorough research before making investment decisions, and be aware of potential risks in different asset classes or industries.

5. Regular Financial Check-ups: Schedule regular check-ups to review your financial situation, evaluate your progress, and make necessary adjustments. This allows you to proactively identify any potential risks or areas of improvement.

Understanding the Psychology behind Wise Financial Decisions: The psychological aspect of finance plays a significant role in making wise financial decisions. Here are some insights to help you navigate the psychological factors that impact your financial choices:

1. Emotion vs. Rationality: Be aware of emotional biases that can cloud your judgment when it comes to money. Avoid making impulsive decisions based on fear, greed, or other emotional triggers. Instead, approach financial decisions with rationality and consider the long-term implications.

2. Delayed Gratification: Cultivate the ability to delay gratification and prioritize long-term financial goals

over short-term desires. This involves making choices that align with your financial well-being, even if they require sacrifices in the present.

3. Seek Knowledge and Education: Continuously educate yourself about personal finance, investment strategies, and risk management. The more knowledge and understanding you have, the better equipped you'll be to make informed decisions and overcome psychological biases.

In Conclusion: Congratulations, dear reader, on exploring the essential aspects of navigating debt and financial risks. By managing debt effectively, mitigating financial risks, and protecting your assets, you are taking important steps toward securing your financial well-being and building long-term wealth.

Remember, effective debt management involves strategic planning, prioritization, and disciplined repayment. Mitigating financial risks requires careful assessment, adequate insurance coverage, and proactive risk management. Understanding the psychological aspects of financial decision-making empowers you to make rational choices aligned with your long-term financial goals.

May your journey toward financial stability and risk management be filled with confidence, resilience, and the knowledge necessary to protect and grow your wealth.

CHAPTER 7: DEVELOPING AN ENTREPRENEURIAL MINDSET

"Entrepreneurship is living a few years of your life like most people won't, so that you can spend the rest of your life like most people can't." - Unknown

Introduction: Welcome, dear reader, to the inspiring chapter dedicated to developing an entrepreneurial mindset. In this chapter, we will explore the world of entrepreneurship, uncover entrepreneurial opportunities, and discuss strategies for starting and scaling a business. By embracing an entrepreneurial mindset, you can unlock your potential, overcome obstacles, and embark on a fulfilling journey of creating wealth and making a meaningful impact.

Exploring Entrepreneurial Opportunities: Entrepreneurship offers exciting opportunities for those who are willing to take risks, innovate, and pursue their passions. Here are strategies to help you identify and explore entrepreneurial opportunities:

1. Self-Reflection: Begin by reflecting on your skills, interests, and passions. Identify areas where you have expertise or a strong desire to make a difference. Look for problems or challenges that you are passionate about

solving.

2. Market Research: Conduct thorough market research to understand current trends, consumer needs, and potential gaps in the market. Identify opportunities where your skills and passions intersect with market demand.

3. Problem Solving: Seek opportunities to provide innovative solutions to existing problems or improve upon existing products or services. Look for inefficiencies, pain points, or underserved customer segments that you can address with your entrepreneurial venture.

Strategies for Starting and Scaling a Business: Once you've identified an entrepreneurial opportunity, it's time to consider strategies for starting and scaling a business. Here are key steps to guide you on this journey:

1. Business Plan: Develop a comprehensive business plan that outlines your vision, mission, target market, product or service offering, marketing strategies, financial projections, and growth plans. A well-thought-out business plan serves as a roadmap for your entrepreneurial venture.

2. Validate Your Idea: Test your business idea by seeking feedback from potential customers, conducting pilot programs, or creating prototypes. Validate the market demand and refine your offering based on customer feedback.

3. Build a Strong Team: Surround yourself with a talented and dedicated team that shares your vision and complements your skills. Hire individuals who are passionate, knowledgeable, and committed to the success of your venture. Leverage their expertise to accelerate growth and overcome challenges.

4. Secure Funding: Explore different funding options to support your business's start-up and growth phases. This may include bootstrapping, seeking angel investors, applying for grants, or obtaining loans. Develop a compelling business case and financial projections to attract potential investors or lenders.

5. Marketing and Branding: Develop a strong brand identity and implement effective marketing strategies to reach your target audience. Leverage both traditional and digital marketing channels to create awareness, build a customer base, and establish a competitive presence.

6. Adapt and Innovate: Stay agile and adaptable in a dynamic business environment. Continuously monitor market trends, customer feedback, and industry developments. Embrace innovation and be willing to iterate and evolve your products, services, and strategies based on changing market demands.

Overcoming Obstacles and Embracing the Entrepreneurial Journey: The entrepreneurial journey is not without its challenges. However, with the right mindset and strategies, you can overcome obstacles and embrace the rewards of entrepreneurship. Here are strategies to help you navigate the journey:

1. Embrace Failure as Learning: View failures and setbacks as learning opportunities. Adopt a growth mindset and understand that challenges are an inherent part of the entrepreneurial journey. Learn from failures, adapt your strategies, and persevere with resilience.

2. Seek Mentors and Networks: Surround yourself with mentors, advisors, and like-minded individuals who can provide guidance, support, and valuable insights. Join entrepreneurial networks, attend industry events, and participate in communities that foster collaboration

and knowledge-sharing.

3. Continual Learning: Commit to lifelong learning and personal development. Stay updated on industry trends, emerging technologies, and best practices. Invest in your knowledge and skill development to stay ahead of the curve and fuel your entrepreneurial success.

In Conclusion: Congratulations, dear reader, on exploring the world of entrepreneurship and developing an entrepreneurial mindset. By identifying entrepreneurial opportunities, implementing strategies for starting and scaling a business, and embracing the challenges and rewards of the entrepreneurial journey, you are paving the way for wealth creation and personal fulfillment.

Remember, entrepreneurship requires passion, dedication, and a willingness to take calculated risks. Be open to new ideas, embrace innovation, and surround yourself with a supportive network. Through perseverance, continuous learning, and a resilient entrepreneurial spirit, you can create a thriving business and make a lasting impact on the world around you.

May your entrepreneurial journey be filled with boundless opportunities, growth, and the fulfillment that comes from turning your dreams into reality.

CHAPTER 8: CULTIVATING A WEALTHY LIFESTYLE

"Money is only a tool. It will take you wherever you wish, but it will not replace you as the driver." - Ayn Rand

Introduction: Welcome, dear reader, to the enlightening chapter dedicated to cultivating a wealthy lifestyle. In this chapter, we will explore strategies for balancing wealth creation with personal well-being, implementing sustainable wealth and legacy planning, and making a positive impact on others. By cultivating a wealthy lifestyle, you can achieve financial success while experiencing fulfillment, joy, and a sense of purpose.

Balancing Wealth Creation with Personal Well-Being: While pursuing wealth creation, it is vital to maintain a balance with personal well-being. Here are strategies to help you achieve this balance:

1. Define Your Definition of Success: Reflect on what success means to you beyond financial achievements. Consider your health, relationships, personal growth, and overall well-being. Define your own metrics of success and align your wealth creation journey with your holistic life goals.

2. Prioritize Self-Care: Make self-care a priority in your life.

Prioritize activities that nourish your physical, mental, and emotional well-being. Take time for exercise, relaxation, hobbies, and quality time with loved ones. Remember, true wealth encompasses more than just financial abundance.

3. Set Boundaries: Establish healthy boundaries between work and personal life. Create dedicated time for yourself, your family, and activities that bring you joy and fulfillment. Avoid falling into the trap of excessive work or neglecting important aspects of your life in pursuit of wealth.

Strategies for Sustainable Wealth and Legacy Planning: Creating sustainable wealth involves prudent financial management and legacy planning. Here are strategies to ensure the long-term sustainability of your wealth:

1. Diversify Your Investments: Spread your investments across different asset classes, industries, and geographical locations. Diversification helps reduce risk and increases the likelihood of long-term returns. Regularly review and rebalance your investment portfolio to align with your risk tolerance and changing market conditions.

2. Estate Planning: Develop a comprehensive estate plan to protect and distribute your wealth according to your wishes. Consult with legal and financial professionals to create a will, establish trusts, and designate beneficiaries. Estate planning ensures the smooth transfer of assets and minimizes potential conflicts.

3. Philanthropic Endeavors: Incorporate philanthropy into your wealth-building journey. Identify causes and organizations that align with your values and make a positive impact. Consider donating money, time, or expertise to support charitable initiatives. Philanthropy brings fulfillment and leaves a lasting legacy beyond

financial wealth.

Giving Back and Making a Positive Impact: True wealth is not just about personal gain; it involves making a positive impact on others and society. Here are strategies to incorporate giving back into your wealth-building journey:

1. Volunteer and Mentoring: Contribute your time and skills to charitable organizations, community projects, or mentorship programs. Sharing your knowledge and experiences can have a profound impact on the lives of others and create a ripple effect of positive change.

2. Social Entrepreneurship: Explore opportunities to create businesses or initiatives that address social or environmental challenges. By combining entrepreneurship with a social mission, you can generate financial success while making a positive impact on the world.

3. Responsible Investing: Consider investing in companies that align with your values and have a positive environmental, social, and governance (ESG) impact. By supporting responsible businesses, you can use your investment dollars to drive positive change.

In Conclusion: Congratulations, dear reader, on exploring the strategies for cultivating a wealthy lifestyle. By balancing wealth creation with personal well-being, implementing sustainable wealth and legacy planning, and making a positive impact on others, you can achieve holistic success and fulfillment.

Remember, true wealth encompasses more than just financial abundance. Prioritize self-care, set boundaries, and define your own metrics of success. Engage in sustainable wealth and legacy planning to ensure the long-term viability of your wealth. Embrace philanthropy and social impact initiatives to make a positive difference in the world.

May your journey towards a wealthy lifestyle be guided by your values, purpose, and a commitment to creating a better world for yourself and others.

CHAPTER 9: STAYING MOTIVATED AND OVERCOMING OBSTACLES

"Obstacles are those frightful things you see when you take your eyes off your goals." - Henry Ford

Introduction: Welcome, dear reader, to the empowering chapter dedicated to staying motivated and overcoming obstacles on your journey to wealth mastery. In this chapter, we will explore strategies for maintaining focus and motivation, dealing with setbacks and financial challenges, and cultivating resilience and perseverance. By developing a strong mindset and overcoming obstacles, you can navigate the ups and downs of your financial journey with unwavering determination.

Strategies for Maintaining Focus and Motivation: Maintaining focus and motivation is crucial for achieving long-term financial success. Here are strategies to help you stay motivated on your wealth mastery journey:

1. Set Clear and Meaningful Goals: Define clear and meaningful financial goals that inspire and motivate you. Ensure your goals are specific, measurable, achievable, relevant, and time-bound (SMART). Regularly revisit and refine your goals to stay aligned

with your vision.

2. Create a Vision Board: Visualize your financial goals by creating a vision board. Gather images, quotes, and symbols that represent your desired outcomes. Place your vision board in a prominent location where you can see it daily, allowing it to serve as a constant reminder of your aspirations.

3. Celebrate Milestones: Celebrate and acknowledge your progress along the way. Break your long-term goals into smaller milestones and reward yourself as you achieve them. Celebrating milestones provides a sense of accomplishment and fuels your motivation to keep moving forward.

Dealing with Setbacks and Financial Challenges: Setbacks and financial challenges are inevitable on the path to wealth mastery. Here are strategies to help you navigate and overcome them:

1. Embrace a Growth Mindset: Adopt a growth mindset that views setbacks and challenges as opportunities for learning and growth. Embrace the belief that you can learn from failures and use them as stepping stones toward success. Shift your perspective to see obstacles as temporary roadblocks rather than permanent barriers.

2. Learn from Setbacks: Reflect on setbacks and extract valuable lessons from them. Identify what went wrong, analyze the factors that contributed to the setback, and develop strategies to prevent similar situations in the future. Use setbacks as opportunities to refine your approach and improve your financial decision-making.

3. Seek Support and Guidance: Reach out for support during challenging times. Connect with mentors, advisors, or a supportive network who can offer guidance, encouragement, and perspective. Their insights and experiences can provide valuable insights and help you overcome obstacles more effectively.

Cultivating Resilience and Perseverance: Resilience and perseverance are key attributes for overcoming obstacles on your wealth mastery journey. Here are strategies to cultivate these qualities:

1. Develop Emotional Resilience: Cultivate emotional resilience by practicing self-care, stress management techniques, and mindfulness. Engage in activities that promote emotional well-being, such as exercise, meditation, journaling, or spending time in nature. Building emotional resilience equips you to handle challenges with a positive mindset.

2. Reframe Challenges as Opportunities: Reframe challenges as opportunities for personal and financial growth. Embrace the mindset that obstacles provide valuable lessons and opportunities for innovation. By reframing challenges, you can approach them with a solution-oriented mindset, fueling your perseverance.

3. Stay Committed to Your Vision: Revisit your vision and remind yourself of the reasons why you embarked on your wealth mastery journey. Visualize the life of abundance and financial freedom you are striving for. Let your vision serve as a source of motivation and a reminder of the ultimate rewards of your efforts.

In Conclusion: Congratulations, dear reader, on exploring strategies for staying motivated and overcoming obstacles on your wealth mastery journey. By maintaining focus and motivation, dealing with setbacks and financial challenges, and cultivating resilience and perseverance, you are building the inner strength necessary to overcome any obstacles that come your way.

Remember, setbacks and challenges are opportunities for growth and learning. Embrace a growth mindset, seek support when needed, and stay committed to your vision. With unwavering determination and resilience, you can overcome obstacles and continue progressing towards your financial goals.

May your journey be filled with the strength to overcome obstacles, the motivation to stay focused, and the perseverance to achieve the wealth and abundance you desire.

CHAPTER 10: THE JOURNEY TO FINANCIAL FREEDOM

"Financial freedom is not a dream. It is an achievable goal that starts with a clear roadmap and a commitment to taking consistent action." - Unknown

Introduction: Welcome, dear reader, to the transformative chapter dedicated to the journey to financial freedom. In this chapter, we will explore the steps to create a personalized roadmap to financial freedom, celebrate milestones along the way, and draw inspiration from the stories of individuals who have achieved financial abundance. By embracing this journey, you can break free from financial constraints and live life on your own terms.

Creating a Personalized Roadmap to Financial Freedom: Financial freedom is a state where you have the resources and flexibility to live life on your own terms, without the constraints of financial stress. Here are steps to create a personalized roadmap to financial freedom:

1. Define Your Financial Independence Number: Calculate your financial independence number, which represents the amount of money required to cover your living expenses without relying on traditional employment. This number serves as a target to strive for and helps you understand how much wealth you need to achieve

financial freedom.

2. Assess Your Current Financial Situation: Evaluate your current financial position by examining your income, expenses, assets, liabilities, and investments. Determine your net worth and identify areas for improvement. This assessment provides a starting point for your journey to financial freedom.

3. Set Clear Financial Goals: Define clear and specific financial goals that align with your vision of financial freedom. These goals may include debt elimination, building an emergency fund, investing for retirement, or creating passive income streams. Set milestones and timelines to track your progress.

4. Develop a Savings and Investment Strategy: Create a savings and investment strategy that allows you to allocate a portion of your income toward achieving your financial goals. Consider different investment vehicles, such as stocks, bonds, real estate, or business ventures, and diversify your portfolio to mitigate risk.

5. Implement Budgeting and Financial Discipline: Establish a budget that aligns with your financial goals and priorities. Track your expenses, cut unnecessary costs, and save consistently. Practice financial discipline by making conscious spending choices and avoiding debt that hinders your progress.

Celebrating Milestones and Measuring Success: As you progress on your journey to financial freedom, it is essential to celebrate milestones and measure your success. Here are strategies to keep you motivated and inspired:

1. Track Your Progress: Regularly review and track your financial progress. Monitor your savings, investments, and debt reduction efforts. Use financial tracking tools or spreadsheets to visualize your progress and understand how far you've come.

2. Celebrate Achievements: Celebrate each milestone you achieve along the way. Recognize the effort and dedication you've put into your financial journey. Treat yourself to a small reward or acknowledge your achievements in meaningful ways that keep you motivated and excited about the next steps.

3. Adjust and Refine Your Roadmap: Continuously review and adjust your roadmap as circumstances change. Your financial goals and priorities may evolve over time, and it's important to stay flexible and adaptable. Regularly assess your progress, make necessary adjustments, and set new targets to continue moving forward.

Inspiring Stories of Financial Abundance: Drawing inspiration from others who have achieved financial abundance can fuel your own journey to financial freedom. Here are stories of individuals who have successfully achieved financial abundance through different paths:

1. Entrepreneurial Success: Learn from the stories of entrepreneurs who have built successful businesses and created significant wealth. Understand their mindset, strategies, and the challenges they overcame on their entrepreneurial journey.

2. Investment Mastery: Explore the stories of individuals who have achieved financial independence through astute investment strategies. Gain insights into their investment philosophies, risk management techniques, and long-term wealth accumulation approaches.

3. Passive Income Ventures: Discover stories of individuals who have created passive income streams, such as rental properties, dividend-paying investments, or online businesses. Understand how they generated passive income and diversified their income sources.

In Conclusion: Congratulations, dear reader, on embarking on the transformative journey to financial freedom. By creating a personalized roadmap, celebrating milestones, and drawing inspiration from others, you are setting yourself up for a life of financial abundance and independence.

Stay committed to your financial goals, adapt your roadmap as needed, and take consistent action. Remember, financial freedom is an achievable goal, and with perseverance and dedication, you can break free from financial constraints and live life on your own terms.

May your journey be filled with milestones to celebrate, continuous progress, and the joy of achieving financial freedom.

CHAPTER 11: HARNESSING THE POWER OF NETWORKING AND RELATIONSHIPS

"Your network is your net worth." - Porter Gale

Introduction: Welcome, dear reader, to the empowering chapter dedicated to harnessing the power of networking and relationships on your journey to financial abundance. In this chapter, we will explore the importance of building a strong professional network, leveraging relationships for financial opportunities, and implementing effective networking strategies for wealth creation. By nurturing meaningful connections, you can open doors to new possibilities and accelerate your path to success.

Building a Strong Professional Network: A strong professional network is a valuable asset on your journey to financial abundance. Here are strategies to build and cultivate a robust network:

1. Define Your Network: Identify the types of individuals you want to connect with based on your financial goals and aspirations. Look for professionals in your industry,

successful entrepreneurs, mentors, investors, and individuals with diverse backgrounds and expertise. Focus on building relationships with people who can provide guidance, support, and potential financial opportunities.

2. Attend Industry Events and Conferences: Participate in industry events, conferences, seminars, and workshops to meet like-minded individuals and expand your network. Engage in conversations, ask thoughtful questions, and actively seek opportunities to connect with others. Networking events provide fertile ground for building valuable relationships.

3. Utilize Online Networking Platforms: Leverage online networking platforms such as LinkedIn, industry-specific forums, and social media groups to connect with professionals in your field. Engage in discussions, share insights, and establish yourself as a valuable contributor in your industry. Online platforms offer a convenient way to connect with individuals globally and expand your network beyond geographical limitations.

Leveraging Relationships for Financial Opportunities: Building relationships is not just about expanding your network; it is about leveraging those connections for financial opportunities. Here are strategies to leverage your relationships effectively:

1. Nurture Authentic Connections: Focus on building genuine, mutually beneficial relationships. Be authentic, listen attentively, and show a genuine interest in others. Offer support, share resources, and be willing to help others without expecting immediate returns. Nurturing authentic connections builds trust and opens doors to potential financial opportunities.

2. Seek Collaborations and Partnerships: Look for opportunities to collaborate with individuals or

businesses that complement your skills, products, or services. Strategic collaborations and partnerships can expand your reach, unlock new markets, and create additional revenue streams. Seek mutually beneficial partnerships that align with your financial goals.

3. Ask for Referrals and Recommendations: Don't be afraid to ask your network for referrals or recommendations. Let them know about the specific financial opportunities you are seeking, such as investment opportunities, clients, or business partnerships. Your network can provide valuable introductions and referrals that can accelerate your path to financial success.

Effective Networking Strategies for Wealth Creation: Networking is an art, and implementing effective strategies can maximize its impact on your wealth creation journey. Here are strategies to enhance your networking efforts:

1. Be Proactive and Consistent: Take a proactive approach to networking by reaching out, following up, and maintaining regular communication with your connections. Be consistent in nurturing relationships and demonstrating your commitment to adding value. Networking is an ongoing process, so invest time and effort into building and maintaining your network.

2. Provide Value: Look for opportunities to provide value to your network. Share valuable insights, resources, or introductions that can benefit others. By being a valuable resource and connector, you position yourself as a trusted and respected member of your network.

3. Attend Networking Events with a Purpose: When attending networking events, set clear intentions and objectives. Identify specific individuals you want to connect with, topics you want to discuss, or information you want to gather. Approach events with

a purpose, and use your time wisely to maximize the impact of your networking efforts.

In Conclusion: Congratulations, dear reader, on understanding the power of networking and relationships in your journey to financial abundance. By building a strong professional network, leveraging relationships for financial opportunities, and implementing effective networking strategies, you are creating a powerful support system that can propel your success.

Remember, networking is not just about expanding your contacts; it is about nurturing meaningful connections and providing value to others. Stay proactive, consistent, and authentic in your networking efforts, and be open to the possibilities that can arise from your relationships.

May your network be a source of inspiration, collaboration, and financial opportunities as you continue on your path to wealth creation and financial abundance.

CHAPTER 12: THE PSYCHOLOGY OF WEALTH AND SUCCESS

"Your thoughts and beliefs shape your reality. Embrace a mindset of abundance and success to unlock your true potential." - Unknown

Introduction: Welcome, dear reader, to the enlightening chapter dedicated to exploring the psychology of wealth and success. In this chapter, we will delve into the mindset and behaviors of successful individuals, overcoming self-sabotage and fear of success, and embracing a growth mindset for continuous personal and financial growth. By understanding the psychology behind wealth and success, you can unlock your true potential and create a life of abundance.

Examining the Mindset and Behaviors of Successful Individuals: Successful individuals possess certain mindset and behaviors that contribute to their achievements. Here are key elements to examine and cultivate:

1. Positive Beliefs about Money: Successful individuals hold positive beliefs about money and abundance. They see money as a tool for growth, impact, and fulfillment. They believe that they are deserving of wealth and capable of creating it through their skills, talents, and efforts. Cultivate positive beliefs about money and align your thoughts with abundance.

2. Persistence and Resilience: Successful individuals demonstrate persistence and resilience in the face of challenges and setbacks. They view failures as stepping stones to success and learn from them. Develop a resilient mindset that allows you to bounce back from setbacks, persevere in the face of adversity, and keep moving forward on your wealth mastery journey.

3. Continuous Learning and Growth: Successful individuals have a thirst for knowledge and a commitment to continuous learning and growth. They invest in their personal and professional development, stay updated on industry trends, and seek out new opportunities. Embrace a growth mindset, be open to new ideas, and actively seek ways to expand your knowledge and skills.

Overcoming Self-Sabotage and Fear of Success: Self-sabotage and fear of success can hinder your progress on the path to wealth and success. Here are strategies to overcome these obstacles:

1. Identify Limiting Beliefs: Reflect on any limiting beliefs you have about wealth, success, and your own abilities. Common limiting beliefs include thoughts like "I'm not deserving of wealth" or "I'm not capable of achieving financial success." Challenge these beliefs and replace them with positive and empowering thoughts that support your growth and abundance.

2. Embrace Self-Worth and Confidence: Cultivate a deep sense of self-worth and confidence in your ability to achieve financial success. Recognize your unique strengths, talents, and experiences that contribute to your potential for wealth creation. Practice positive self-talk, affirmations, and visualization techniques to boost your self-worth and confidence.

3. Take Action Despite Fear: Fear of success can paralyze you and prevent you from taking necessary actions.

Embrace the discomfort and take action anyway. Start with small steps, gradually expanding your comfort zone. Each action you take builds momentum and strengthens your belief in your ability to achieve financial success.

Embracing a Growth Mindset for Continuous Personal and Financial Growth: A growth mindset is the belief that your abilities and intelligence can be developed through dedication and hard work. Embrace a growth mindset for continuous personal and financial growth:

1. Embrace Challenges as Opportunities: View challenges as opportunities for growth and learning. Instead of shying away from difficult tasks, approach them with a positive attitude and a willingness to learn. Embrace challenges as stepping stones toward your financial goals.

2. Seek Feedback and Learn from Mistakes: Actively seek feedback from mentors, peers, and experts in your field. Embrace constructive criticism as an opportunity to improve and grow. Learn from your mistakes and see them as valuable lessons on your journey to financial success.

3. Cultivate a Curious and Open Mind: Cultivate a curious and open mind that is receptive to new ideas, perspectives, and opportunities. Be open to change, embrace innovation, and stay curious about emerging trends and technologies. A curious mind is essential for staying ahead in an evolving economy.

In Conclusion: Congratulations, dear reader, on delving into the psychology of wealth and success. By examining the mindset and behaviors of successful individuals, overcoming self-sabotage and fear of success, and embracing a growth mindset, you are unlocking your true potential for personal and financial growth.

Remember, your thoughts and beliefs shape your reality. Embrace positive beliefs about money, cultivate resilience in the face of challenges, and adopt a growth mindset for continuous learning and growth. With the right mindset, you can overcome obstacles, achieve financial success, and create a life of abundance.

May you embrace the power of your mind, cultivate empowering beliefs, and continue to evolve on your journey to financial mastery and personal fulfillment.

CHAPTER 13: CREATING A PERSONAL BRAND FOR FINANCIAL SUCCESS

"Your personal brand is a reflection of your values, expertise, and unique qualities. Build a strong personal brand to attract financial success and create opportunities." - Unknown

Introduction: Welcome, dear reader, to the insightful chapter dedicated to creating a personal brand for financial success. In this chapter, we will explore the importance of personal branding in wealth creation, building an online presence, leveraging social media, and positioning yourself as an expert or authority in your field. By developing a strong personal brand, you can attract financial opportunities, establish credibility, and unlock new pathways to success.

Understanding the Importance of Personal Branding in Wealth Creation: Personal branding is the process of deliberately shaping and managing your professional image and reputation. It involves establishing a unique identity and showcasing your expertise, values, and unique qualities. Here's why personal branding is crucial for wealth creation:

1. Differentiation in a Competitive Market: In a crowded marketplace, a strong personal brand sets you apart from the competition. It allows you to showcase your unique value proposition and differentiate yourself in the eyes of potential clients, investors, or business partners.

2. Building Trust and Credibility: A well-crafted personal brand builds trust and credibility with your target audience. By consistently delivering value, demonstrating expertise, and maintaining a strong online presence, you establish yourself as a trusted authority in your field. Trust and credibility are vital for attracting financial opportunities.

3. Attracting Financial Opportunities: A strong personal brand attracts financial opportunities such as clients, investors, partnerships, speaking engagements, or media features. When you are known for your expertise and have a clear personal brand, people are more likely to seek out your services or collaborate with you, leading to increased financial success.

Building an Online Presence and Leveraging Social Media: In today's digital age, building an online presence is crucial for personal branding and attracting financial success. Here are strategies for building your online presence and leveraging social media effectively:

1. Define Your Online Identity: Clearly define your professional identity, values, and areas of expertise. Develop a compelling personal brand statement that communicates who you are, what you do, and the value you provide. Ensure consistency across all online platforms.

2. Create a Professional Website: Establish a professional website that serves as your online hub. Showcase your

expertise, share valuable content, and provide contact information for potential clients or collaborators. Your website should reflect your personal brand and be user-friendly.

3. Utilize Social Media Platforms: Choose social media platforms that align with your target audience and industry. Consistently share valuable content, engage with your audience, and build relationships. Utilize features such as LinkedIn articles, Facebook groups, or Twitter chats to establish yourself as an industry thought leader.

4. Share Valuable Content: Regularly create and share high-quality content that aligns with your personal brand and resonates with your target audience. This could include blog articles, videos, podcasts, or infographics. Demonstrate your expertise and provide value to your audience.

Positioning Yourself as an Expert or Authority in Your Field: To attract financial success, positioning yourself as an expert or authority in your field is crucial. Here are strategies to establish yourself as a thought leader:

1. Share Your Knowledge and Expertise: Share your knowledge generously through public speaking engagements, webinars, or workshops. Contribute to industry publications, write guest blog posts, or host your own podcast. Position yourself as a go-to resource for valuable insights and expertise.

2. Engage in Thought Leadership Activities: Actively participate in industry conferences, panel discussions, or networking events. Seek opportunities to share your expertise and showcase your unique perspective on industry-related topics. Establish yourself as a thought leader by providing innovative ideas and solutions.

3. Seek Collaborations and Partnerships: Collaborate with

other industry experts, influencers, or complementary businesses. Jointly create content, host webinars, or collaborate on projects that showcase your expertise. Collaborations and partnerships amplify your reach and reinforce your position as an authority in your field.

In Conclusion: Congratulations, dear reader, on recognizing the importance of creating a personal brand for financial success. By building a strong personal brand, establishing an online presence, leveraging social media, and positioning yourself as an expert or authority in your field, you are opening doors to new financial opportunities and attracting success.

Remember, your personal brand is a reflection of your values, expertise, and unique qualities. Be intentional in shaping and managing your brand, consistently provide value, and demonstrate your expertise. With a strong personal brand, you can elevate your professional reputation, attract financial success, and create lasting impact.

May you embark on the journey of personal branding with confidence, authenticity, and a commitment to continuous growth. Embrace the power of your personal brand and watch as it opens doors to new possibilities on your path to financial success.

CHAPTER 14: MAXIMIZING TAX EFFICIENCY AND WEALTH PRESERVATION

"Pay yourself first, but don't forget to pay the taxman wisely." - Unknown

Introduction: Welcome, dear reader, to the informative chapter dedicated to maximizing tax efficiency and wealth preservation. In this chapter, we will explore strategies for legally minimizing tax obligations, understanding tax-efficient investment vehicles, and protecting and preserving your wealth for future generations. By optimizing your tax strategy and implementing effective wealth preservation techniques, you can enhance your financial well-being and create a lasting legacy.

Strategies for Minimizing Tax Obligations: Minimizing your tax obligations is a key aspect of wealth mastery. Here are strategies to help you maximize tax efficiency:

1. Understand Tax Laws and Regulations: Stay informed about tax laws and regulations in your jurisdiction. Familiarize yourself with allowable deductions, exemptions, and credits that can help reduce your tax

liability. Consider consulting with a tax professional to ensure you are maximizing your tax benefits.

2. Contribute to Tax-Advantaged Accounts: Take advantage of tax-advantaged accounts such as retirement accounts (e.g., 401(k), IRA) or health savings accounts (HSA). Contributions to these accounts are often tax-deductible or tax-free, allowing you to reduce your taxable income and potentially grow your investments tax-deferred or tax-free.

3. Optimize Deductions and Credits: Identify eligible deductions and credits to reduce your tax liability. This may include deductions for mortgage interest, student loan interest, charitable contributions, or educational expenses. Keep thorough records and consult with a tax professional to ensure you are maximizing your deductions and credits.

Understanding Tax-Efficient Investment Vehicles: Investing in tax-efficient vehicles can help you preserve and grow your wealth while minimizing tax implications. Consider the following options:

1. Tax-Advantaged Retirement Accounts: Contribute to retirement accounts that offer tax advantages, such as 401(k)s or IRAs. These accounts often provide tax-deferred growth or tax-free withdrawals in retirement, allowing your investments to grow more efficiently over time.

2. Municipal Bonds: Consider investing in municipal bonds, which offer tax advantages. Interest earned from municipal bonds is often tax-free at the federal level and may also be exempt from state or local taxes, depending on where you reside.

3. Tax-Efficient Funds: Look for tax-efficient investment funds, such as index funds or exchange-traded funds (ETFs), which are designed to minimize

taxable distributions. These funds typically have lower turnover and generate fewer capital gains, helping you minimize tax obligations.

Protecting and Preserving Your Wealth: Preserving your wealth for future generations requires thoughtful planning and implementation of various strategies. Consider the following techniques:

1. Estate Planning: Work with an estate planning attorney to develop a comprehensive estate plan that reflects your wishes and minimizes estate taxes. This may include creating a will, establishing trusts, and assigning beneficiaries for your assets. Regularly review and update your estate plan to accommodate changing circumstances.

2. Asset Protection: Implement asset protection strategies to safeguard your wealth from potential risks or legal liabilities. This may involve structuring your assets through legal entities such as trusts, limited liability companies (LLCs), or family limited partnerships (FLPs). Asset protection techniques can provide a layer of defense against unforeseen events.

3. Charitable Giving and Philanthropy: Consider incorporating philanthropy into your wealth-building journey. Charitable giving allows you to make a positive impact while potentially offering tax advantages, such as deductibility for charitable contributions. Explore avenues for supporting causes you care about and leaving a meaningful legacy.

In Conclusion: Congratulations, dear reader, on exploring strategies to maximize tax efficiency and preserve your wealth. By minimizing tax obligations, understanding tax-efficient investment vehicles, and implementing effective wealth preservation techniques, you are setting the foundation for long-term financial security and creating a lasting legacy.

Remember, staying informed about tax laws, optimizing deductions and credits, and leveraging tax-advantaged accounts are essential for minimizing your tax liability. Additionally, investing in tax-efficient vehicles and implementing asset protection and estate planning strategies will help preserve your wealth for future generations.

May you navigate the intricacies of tax efficiency and wealth preservation with confidence and seek guidance from professionals when needed. By optimizing your tax strategy and safeguarding your wealth, you can enjoy the fruits of your labor while creating a meaningful impact for yourself and future generations.

CHAPTER 15:
EMBRACING THE DIGITAL ECONOMY AND TECHNOLOGICAL DISRUPTION

"Embrace technology and the digital economy to unlock new opportunities for wealth creation and stay ahead in an ever-evolving world." - Unknown

Introduction: Welcome, dear reader, to the dynamic chapter dedicated to embracing the digital economy and technological disruption. In this chapter, we will explore the opportunities presented by the digital landscape, harnessing technology for wealth creation, and adapting to changes in an evolving economy. By embracing technology and the digital economy, you can unlock new pathways to financial success and stay ahead in a rapidly changing world.

Exploring Opportunities in the Digital Landscape: The digital landscape has revolutionized the way we live, work, and do business. Embracing the digital economy opens doors to new opportunities for wealth creation. Consider the following avenues:

1. Online Business and E-commerce: Start or expand an

online business to leverage the global reach of the internet. E-commerce platforms enable you to sell products or services to a wide customer base, with reduced overhead costs and the potential for scalability.

2. Digital Products and Services: Create and sell digital products or services, such as e-books, online courses, software, or digital art. The digital realm offers immense potential for monetizing your expertise and intellectual property.

3. Freelancing and Remote Work: Embrace the flexibility and global connectivity offered by remote work and freelancing. Leverage your skills to offer freelance services to clients worldwide or explore remote work opportunities in various industries.

Harnessing Technology for Wealth Creation: Technological advancements have paved the way for innovative wealth creation strategies. Here are ways to harness technology effectively:

1. Automation and Outsourcing: Embrace automation and outsourcing to streamline processes and free up your time for higher-value activities. Automate repetitive tasks, utilize software and tools, and consider outsourcing non-core functions to focus on income-generating activities.

2. Digital Marketing and Social Media: Utilize digital marketing techniques and social media platforms to reach and engage with your target audience. Leverage the power of online advertising, content marketing, search engine optimization (SEO), and social media campaigns to promote your brand and attract customers.

3. Data Analysis and Artificial Intelligence: Embrace the power of data analysis and artificial intelligence (AI) to gain insights and make informed business decisions. Utilize data analytics tools to identify trends, optimize

strategies, and personalize customer experiences.

Adapting to Changes and Staying Ahead: In an ever-evolving economy, the ability to adapt and stay ahead is crucial for financial success. Consider the following strategies:

1. Continuous Learning and Skill Development: Embrace a mindset of lifelong learning and commit to continuous skill development. Stay updated on emerging technologies, industry trends, and market changes. Invest in yourself to remain relevant and adaptable in a fast-paced digital world.

2. Networking and Collaboration: Build a strong professional network and seek collaborative opportunities. Engage with industry peers, attend conferences and events, and participate in online communities to stay connected and leverage collective knowledge and resources.

3. Agile Mindset and Innovation: Embrace an agile mindset that embraces change and fosters innovation. Embrace new technologies, experiment with different strategies, and be open to taking calculated risks. Continuously seek opportunities to innovate and disrupt traditional models.

In Conclusion: Congratulations, dear reader, on embracing the digital economy and technological disruption. By exploring opportunities in the digital landscape, harnessing technology for wealth creation, and adapting to changes in an evolving economy, you are positioning yourself for success in the digital era.

Remember, the digital landscape offers abundant opportunities for wealth creation and personal growth. Embrace technology, stay informed about digital trends, and be open to adopting new tools and strategies. Continuously adapt, learn, and innovate to stay ahead in an ever-changing world.

May you navigate the digital economy with confidence, leverage technology to unlock new pathways to financial success, and embrace the exciting possibilities that lie ahead. Embracing the digital era will empower you to thrive in an evolving world of limitless opportunities

CHAPTER 16: MINDFUL SPENDING AND CONSCIOUS CONSUMPTION

"Be mindful of how you spend your money, aligning your purchases with your values and long-term goals to create a meaningful and fulfilling financial life." - Unknown

Introduction: Welcome, dear reader, to the thought-provoking chapter dedicated to mindful spending and conscious consumption. In this chapter, we will explore the importance of cultivating mindful spending habits, distinguishing between needs and wants, and aligning your spending with your values and long-term goals. By practicing mindful spending and conscious consumption, you can create a meaningful and fulfilling financial life.

Cultivating Mindful Spending Habits: Mindful spending involves being intentional and aware of how you allocate your financial resources. Here are strategies to cultivate mindful spending habits:

1. Assess Your Financial Values: Reflect on your values and priorities when it comes to money. Identify what truly matters to you and align your spending

with those values. This awareness will guide your financial decisions and ensure that your money is directed towards what brings you true satisfaction and fulfillment.

2. Practice Delayed Gratification: Before making a purchase, practice delayed gratification. Take time to consider whether the purchase aligns with your long-term goals and if it truly brings value to your life. This pause allows you to make more deliberate and mindful spending choices.

3. Set Spending Limits and Budget: Establish spending limits and create a budget that reflects your financial goals and priorities. Track your expenses regularly and ensure that your spending aligns with your budget. This practice fosters mindfulness and helps you stay accountable to your financial plan.

Distinguishing Between Needs and Wants: Distinguishing between needs and wants is crucial for mindful spending. Here's how to navigate this differentiation:

1. Identify True Needs: Differentiate between essential needs and discretionary wants. True needs include necessities like housing, utilities, food, healthcare, and transportation. Prioritize meeting these needs before indulging in discretionary wants.

2. Question Your Wants: When confronted with a desire to make a purchase, ask yourself if it is truly necessary or if it stems from a fleeting impulse. Challenge yourself to determine whether the purchase aligns with your values and long-term goals.

3. Practice Mindful Consumption: Adopt a conscious approach to consumption by considering the environmental and social impact of your purchases. Opt for sustainable and ethical products and support businesses that align with your values. Mindful

consumption extends beyond personal satisfaction to making choices that benefit the planet and society.

Aligning Spending with Values and Long-Term Goals: Conscious consumption involves aligning your spending with your values and long-term goals. Consider the following strategies:

1. Define Your Financial Goals: Set clear financial goals that align with your values and aspirations. Whether it's saving for retirement, starting a business, or supporting a cause, identify goals that hold personal meaning and significance.

2. Prioritize Your Values: Evaluate how your spending reflects your values. Identify areas where you can align your spending with what truly matters to you. This may involve redirecting funds towards experiences, personal growth, or supporting causes that resonate with your values.

3. Practice Mindful Generosity: Cultivate a mindset of giving and generosity. Allocate a portion of your financial resources to charitable causes or community initiatives that align with your values. Mindful generosity not only benefits others but also contributes to your overall well-being and sense of fulfillment.

In Conclusion: Congratulations, dear reader, on exploring the path of mindful spending and conscious consumption. By cultivating mindful spending habits, distinguishing between needs and wants, and aligning your spending with your values and long-term goals, you can create a meaningful and fulfilling financial life.

Remember, mindful spending involves being intentional and aware of how you allocate your financial resources. Practice delayed gratification, set spending limits, and distinguish between needs and wants. Align your spending with your values and prioritize your financial goals to ensure that your money brings true satisfaction and reflects what truly matters to you.

May you navigate the realm of mindful spending and conscious consumption with wisdom and intention, creating a financial life that aligns with your values and brings you lasting fulfillment.

CHAPTER 17: GIVING AND PHILANTHROPY: THE POWER OF GENEROSITY

"Generosity is not just about giving money; it's about making a difference, leaving a positive impact, and creating a legacy that extends beyond financial wealth." - Unknown

Introduction: Welcome, dear reader, to the inspiring chapter dedicated to the power of generosity, giving, and philanthropy. In this chapter, we will explore the importance of incorporating philanthropy into your wealth-building journey, creating a legacy through charitable giving, and the profound impact that giving has on personal fulfillment and overall well-being. By embracing the power of generosity, you can make a positive difference in the world and experience the true wealth that comes from giving.

Incorporating Philanthropy into Your Wealth-Building Journey: Philanthropy goes beyond financial success. It involves using your resources, skills, and influence to make a positive impact on others and society as a whole. Consider the following strategies for incorporating philanthropy into your wealth-building journey:

1. Define Your Philanthropic Vision: Reflect on the causes,

issues, or communities that resonate with you on a deep level. Identify areas where you can make a meaningful difference and align your philanthropic efforts with your personal values and passions.

2. Allocate Resources: Set aside a portion of your financial resources specifically for philanthropy. Create a giving plan or budget that reflects your philanthropic goals and outlines how you will allocate funds to support causes and organizations aligned with your vision.

3. Volunteer Your Time and Skills: Philanthropy extends beyond financial contributions. Consider volunteering your time, expertise, or skills to support nonprofit organizations or community initiatives. Your knowledge and hands-on involvement can make a significant impact and create meaningful change.

Creating a Legacy through Charitable Giving: Charitable giving allows you to create a lasting legacy that extends beyond financial wealth. Consider the following strategies for creating a meaningful legacy through your philanthropic efforts:

1. Develop a Giving Strategy: Define your giving priorities and develop a strategy that reflects your philanthropic vision and values. Consider the causes, organizations, or projects that you want to support and outline how your giving will create a lasting impact.

2. Establish a Donor-Advised Fund or Foundation: Consider establishing a donor-advised fund or a private foundation to manage your charitable giving. These vehicles provide structure and enable you to have a long-term impact while involving your family and future generations in your philanthropic endeavors.

3. Involve Loved Ones: Engage your family, friends, or loved ones in your philanthropic activities. Encourage shared giving experiences, involve them in the decision-making process, and instill the values of generosity and

compassion in future generations.

The Impact of Giving on Personal Fulfillment and Overall Well-Being: Giving not only benefits others but also brings immense personal fulfillment and overall well-being. Consider the following ways in which giving enhances your life:

1. Sense of Purpose and Meaning: Giving provides a sense of purpose and meaning beyond financial success. Knowing that your resources are making a positive difference in the lives of others brings a deep sense of fulfillment and joy.

2. Connection and Empathy: Giving fosters connection and empathy with others. By supporting causes and organizations, you develop a greater understanding of the challenges faced by others and cultivate compassion and empathy for those in need.

3. Gratitude and Appreciation: Giving cultivates gratitude and appreciation for the blessings in your life. It reminds you of the abundance you possess and encourages a mindset of gratitude, which in turn attracts more positivity and abundance.

In Conclusion: Congratulations, dear reader, on recognizing the power of generosity and incorporating philanthropy into your wealth-building journey. By embracing the act of giving, creating a lasting legacy through charitable contributions, and experiencing the personal fulfillment that comes from making a positive impact, you are enriching your life and the lives of others.

Remember, philanthropy is not limited to financial contributions. It encompasses sharing your time, skills, and resources to create positive change. Align your giving with your values, involve loved ones in your philanthropic endeavors, and embrace the profound impact that generosity brings to your personal fulfillment and overall well-being.

May your journey of giving and philanthropy be a source of joy, inspiration, and a testament to the true wealth that comes from making a positive difference in the world.

CHAPTER 18: STRATEGIES FOR FINANCIAL INDEPENDENCE AND EARLY RETIREMENT

"Financial independence and early retirement are attainable goals with careful planning, disciplined saving, and a commitment to living life on your own terms." - Unknown

Introduction: Welcome, dear reader, to the empowering chapter dedicated to strategies for achieving financial independence and early retirement. In this chapter, we will explore the concept of financial independence, calculate your financial independence number, and delve into strategies that will help you achieve the freedom to live life on your own terms. By implementing these strategies, you can pave the way for a future of financial security and the ability to retire early.

Understanding the Concept of Financial Independence: Financial independence is the state of having sufficient wealth and passive income to cover your expenses, allowing you to maintain your desired lifestyle without relying on employment income. It grants you the freedom to pursue your passions, spend time with loved ones, and make choices based on your values rather than financial obligations.

Calculating Your Financial Independence Number: To pursue financial independence, it is essential to calculate your financial independence number, which represents the amount of wealth you need to achieve your desired level of financial freedom. Consider the following steps:

1. Determine Your Annual Expenses: Analyze your current spending patterns and estimate your annual expenses in retirement. Consider factors such as housing, healthcare, transportation, food, travel, and discretionary spending.

2. Multiply by the Safe Withdrawal Rate: The safe withdrawal rate is the percentage of your investment portfolio that you can withdraw annually without depleting the principal. Commonly, a safe withdrawal rate of 3-4% is used. Multiply your annual expenses by the inverse of the safe withdrawal rate (e.g., divide by 0.03 for a 3% withdrawal rate).

3. Add Contingency and Extra Expenses: Factor in additional expenses, such as unforeseen circumstances, healthcare costs, or desired lifestyle enhancements. Adding a buffer ensures you have financial security and can adapt to unexpected situations.

Strategies for Achieving Early Retirement and Financial Independence: To achieve early retirement and financial independence, consider implementing the following strategies:

1. Save and Invest Aggressively: Adopt a disciplined approach to saving and investing. Strive to save a significant portion of your income and invest it wisely in diversified assets that align with your risk tolerance and goals. Maximize contributions to retirement accounts and take advantage of employer matching programs.

2. Minimize Lifestyle Inflation: Resist the temptation to inflate your lifestyle with increased income. Instead, maintain a frugal mindset and avoid unnecessary expenses. Continually evaluate your spending habits and prioritize saving and investing over short-term gratification.

3. Create Multiple Streams of Income: Diversify your income sources to build resilience and increase your wealth accumulation rate. Explore opportunities for passive income, such as real estate investments, dividends from stocks, or creating an online business that generates income even when you're not actively working.

4. Continuously Educate Yourself: Commit to ongoing financial education and stay informed about personal finance, investing, and wealth-building strategies. Expand your knowledge through books, courses, seminars, and engaging with financial professionals. Strengthening your financial literacy empowers you to make informed decisions and optimize your wealth-building efforts.

5. Monitor and Adjust: Regularly review your financial progress and make necessary adjustments along the way. Assess the performance of your investments, track your expenses, and ensure your savings rate aligns with your financial goals. Stay adaptable and make changes as needed to stay on track towards financial independence.

In Conclusion: Congratulations, dear reader, on exploring the strategies for achieving financial independence and early retirement. By understanding the concept of financial independence, calculating your financial independence number, and implementing strategies such as aggressive saving, prudent investing, and multiple income streams, you are setting yourself up for a future of financial security and the freedom to live life on your own terms.

Remember, achieving financial independence requires discipline, careful planning, and a long-term perspective. Stay committed to your financial goals, adjust as necessary, and embrace the journey towards early retirement and the fulfillment that comes from gaining control over your financial future.

May these strategies pave the way for a life of financial independence, giving you the freedom to pursue your passions, create meaningful experiences, and enjoy the abundance that comes from living life on your own terms.

EMBRACING THE JOURNEY TO ABUNDANCE

Congratulations, dear reader, on reaching the end of this inspiring guide to mastering the art of wealth and unlocking abundance in your life. Throughout these chapters, we have explored the mindset, strategies, and practical techniques necessary to achieve financial success and create a life of true wealth.

Remember, wealth is not merely measured by the number in your bank account but by the richness of experiences, relationships, personal growth, and the positive impact you make on the world. It is about aligning your financial goals with your values, pursuing your passions, and finding joy and fulfillment in the journey.

As you embark on this path to abundance, keep in mind the power of your thoughts, beliefs, and actions. Embrace an abundance mindset, release limiting beliefs, and envision yourself living a life of prosperity and purpose. Let gratitude be your guiding light, appreciating the blessings you have while attracting more blessings into your life.

Stay committed to continuous learning, for knowledge is the key that unlocks doors to new opportunities. Educate yourself about personal finance, investing, and wealth-building strategies. Seek guidance from mentors and surround yourself with individuals who inspire and uplift you on your journey.

Remember, setbacks and challenges are inevitable, but it is in these moments that your resilience and perseverance shine. Embrace each obstacle as an opportunity for growth and learning. Stay motivated, maintain focus, and never lose sight of your financial goals and the abundant life that awaits you.

Lastly, as you progress on your wealth mastery journey, always remember the importance of giving back. Cultivate a spirit of generosity and incorporate philanthropy into your life. Share your blessings with others, make a positive impact, and leave a legacy that extends beyond financial wealth.

Now, dear reader, it is time for you to take what you have learned and put it into action. Embrace the principles and strategies outlined in this guide, adapt them to your unique circumstances, and create a personalized roadmap to financial freedom.

Believe in yourself, for you possess the power to create the life of abundance you desire. Trust in the process, stay focused, and celebrate each milestone along the way. Your journey to wealth mastery is not just about the destination but about the transformation and growth you experience along the path.

May your life be filled with prosperity, joy, and the abundance that comes from living in alignment with your values and purpose. Embrace the art of wealth mastery and unlock the limitless possibilities that await you.